# PSYCHOLINGUISTICS

Joseph A. DeVito

THE BOBBS-MERRILL COMPANY, INC.

*Indianapolis*    *New York*

**The Bobbs-Merrill
studies in
communicative
disorders**

*Series Editor*
HARVEY HALPERN

*Speech Consultant*
RUSSEL R. WINDES

# Psycholinguistics

Unlike Athena who sprung fully grown from the head of Zeus, psycholinguistics developed only gradually. Its progenitors, as its name implies, were psychology and linguistics. When psychologists "realized" that man, the object of their science, unlike the hungry albino rat, spoke and linguists "realized" that language, the object of their science, was spoken by man, the union of these two disciplines was both inevitable and immanent. Psycholinguistics, then, quite logically grew out of the psychological investigations of talking man and linguistic investigations of man's talking.[1]

In 1961 Sol Saporta (p. vi) noted that "psycholinguistics is still an

---

[1] The first major publication in the field was *Psycholinguistics: a survey of theory and research problems*, ed. Charles E. Osgood and Thomas A. Sebeok. It was originally published in 1954 as a supplement to both the *Journal of Abnormal and Social Psychology* and the *International Journal of American Linguistics* in order to reach its two major audiences of psychologists and linguists. It was reissued in paperback in 1965 by Indiana University Press together with A. Richard Diebold's "A survey of psycholinguistic research, 1954–1964"—originally a review essay of Saporta's *Psycholinguistics: a book of readings*—and George A. Miller's "The Psycholinguists: on the new scientists of language." An account of the development of psycholinguistics, together with excerpts from the writings of some of the leading researchers, is provided by Blumenthal (1970). For a provocative discussion of the analysis of verbal behavior, focusing on re-

amorphous field," and in 1966 Susan Ervin-Tripp and Dan Slobin (p. 435) observed that "psycholinguistics appears to be a field in search of a definition." Today, psycholinguistics has still not lost its amorphous quality, nor has it found the definition for which it has been searching; different theorists and researchers have different and often divergent points of view and emphases.[2] Nevertheless, psycholinguistics as a scientific field of study is not difficult to characterize, at least in general terms; among the numerous differences there is still considerable agreement concerning the principal domain if not the precise boundaries.

Psycholinguistics is concerned with two broad and basic questions: 1.) How does the child acquire language? and 2.) How are linguistic units encoded and decoded, produced and understood? Concerned as it is with general mechanisms of language acquisition, production, and understanding, psycholinguistics may be viewed as a metascience or higher order science under which may be grouped the more specific and specialized sciences of language and language behavior (DeVito, in press a). Ultimately, these other disciplines such as acoustics, speech and language pathology, audiology, speech perception, and the like will probably all be subsumed under or absorbed by psycholinguistics.

Since the province of psycholinguistics concerns the general mechanisms of language behavior, it is a science that is logically prior to all other more limited ones which deal with selected and specialized aspects of language behavior. One cannot study disordered language in any meaningful sense without first understanding the structure and function of normal language. One cannot talk intelligently about delayed speech and language without being aware of the normal development of speech and language. One cannot study disturbances in speech perception with any real insight without first understanding the normal processes of speech perception (Ogilvie and DeVito, in press).

Psycholinguistic theories and research findings, therefore, are potentially applicable to any study concerned with language and behavior (cf.,

---

search methodologies, see Williams (1970a). Current research in psycholinguistics is perhaps best represented by the studies appearing in the *Journal of Verbal Learning and Verbal Behavior* (Academic Press). Extensive analytical coverage is provided by *Language and Language Behavior Abstracts* (University of Michigan Center for Research on Language and Language Behavior). References to later works in psycholinguistics are given in note 2.

[2] For some of these different points of view see, for example, Fodor, Jenkins, and Saporta (1967), Markel (1969), Carroll (1964), Jakobovits and Miron (1967), DeVito (1967b, 1970a, in press a), Osgood (1963b), Miller and McNeill (1969), Rommetveit (1968), d'Arcais and Levelt (1970), Hörmann (1971), Slobin (1971), and Fillenbaum (1971).

Rosenberg and Koplin 1968). In some areas these applications have already been made with considerable success. In others the applications are just beginning to be seen. In most areas, however, the applications have not even been explored, the relevant relationships not even hypothesized. Yet, it is likely that in the next few years the impact of this field will be such that it will be impossible for any student to deal competently with any aspect of language behavior without the insights of psycholinguistics.

The first of the major questions concerning psycholinguistics, "How does the child acquire language?" called "developmental psycholinguistics" by David McNeill (1966, 1970) is treated by Paula Menyuk in her paper in this series and in more detail in *The acquisition and development of language* (1971). An extensive bibliography of recent research is provided by DeVito (in press b). The second question, "How are linguistic units encoded and decoded?" which unfortunately does not have a very convenient name (experimental psycholinguistics?), is considered here. The discussion is divided into two major parts. In the first some basics of linguistic and psychological theories are considered, and in the second some psycholinguistic investigations of speech and language behavior concerning hesitation phenomena, phonology, semantics, syntax, style, and language are explored.

*Theories in psycholinguistics*

---

**Linguistic theory**  To survey linguistic theory—the theory that provides the starting place for most psycholinguistic investigations—would be impossible within the confines of one paper. Yet, it is essential that some basic assumptions of contemporary linguistic science be made clear before considering the specific experimental studies.[3]

[3] It is assumed here that the general pattern of language(s) and of grammar(s) proposed by Noam Chomsky is essentially correct. See, for example, Chomsky's *Syntactic structures* (1957) for early formulations and his *Aspects of the theory of syntax* (1965) and *Language and mind* (1968) for more recent accounts. Currently a number of Chomsky's formulations are being challenged and revisions in grammatical theory are being proposed almost daily. Some of the more recent developments are considered in *New horizons in linguistics*, ed. John Lyons (1970). The best way to keep abreast of these developments, however, is to read the linguistics journals, e.g., *Foundations of Language, Journal of Linguistics, Language,* and *Word.* Articles from these and other pertinent journals are abstracted quarterly in *Language and Language Behavior Abstracts.* Those aspects of linguistic science of particular relevance to psycholinguistics are surveyed by Fodor, Jenkins, and Saporta (1967), Miller and McNeill (1969), and DeVito (1970a).

Aside from the complexity of language and of theories of language, the difficulty of presenting any clear description is compounded by the fact that linguistics is undergoing drastic changes. In the early days of psycholinguistics, the structural linguistics of Bloomfield, Trager and Smith, and Fries dominated. In 1957, when Chomsky published his *Syntactic Structures*, the structural linguistics was largely abandoned and transformational grammar took its place. This theory was then substantially revised by Chomsky and his associates in the early 1960s. Today even greater changes are being made.

One of the most obvious facts about language is that it is structured. The symbols which we use to speak cannot be arranged arbitrarily; rather, they must be arranged according to a fixed set of rules, which all native speakers have somehow acquired and which exist on all language levels. It should be stated at the outset that "rules" in linguistics are descriptive statements that attempt to phrase, as simply and as economically as possible, the regularities that occur in language. Linguistic rules, therefore, are not prescriptive or proscriptive—are not concerned with what should or should not be done—but rather are statements describing the structure of language. At the phonemic level we have rules for permissible and non-permissible phoneme sequences. Thus, in English it is permissible to string together the sounds /p/, /l/, and /o/ to form the sequence /plo/ but it is not permissible to form the sequence /lpo/. At the level of morphemes, meaningful units of language, there are also rules for permissible and non-permissible sequences. Thus, it is permissible to add /z/ to form the plural of *boy* but not to form the plural of *cat* which demands /s/. Likewise we can say *the man up the tree* but not *the up the man tree*. That is, there are rules for the combination of bound morphemes—meaningful units which cannot stand alone such as the plural, past tense, or adverbial *-ly* morphemes—as well as for free morphemes—meaningful units which can stand alone such as *the, man, tree*.

Rules for certain permissible sequences can be easily formulated and constitute part of the grammar of English. For example, the rule for the formation of the English plural might be phrased somewhat as follows:

/-ɪz/  for all words ending in groove fricatives and affricates, i.e., /s, z, š, ž, č, ǰ/;
/ -s/  for all words ending in voiceless consonants, i.e., /p, t, k, f, θ/; and
/ -z/  for all other words.

Likewise, we may formulate rules for the conversion of sentences. Taking the simple, active, affirmative, declarative sentence as a base, we may formulate the rule for the formation of negatives, questions, imperatives, and the like. For example, the sentence "The dog chased the boy" can be converted into the yes/no question "Did the dog chase the boy?" by the application of a relatively simple rule. The base sentence may be symbolized as follows:

$det + N_1 + V + past\ tense + det + N_2$.

This would be read as determiner plus noun$_1$ plus verb plus past tense plus determiner plus noun$_2$. The yes/no question may be symbolized as follows:

$aux + past\ tense + det + N_1 + V + det + N_2 + ?$

The rule would simply state the "transformation" that must be applied to the first sentence to yield the second sentence and is normally written as the instructional rule to rewrite Sentence$_1$ as Sentence$_2$. It would appear in the grammar somewhat as follows:

$det + N_1 + V + past\ tense + det + N_2 \longrightarrow aux + past\ tense + det + N_1 + V + det + N_2 + ?$

where the arrow is read as the instructional rule to rewrite the left side as the right side. Technically, rules such as these do not operate on sentences but rather on base structures, which are abstract representations of sentences. The simple, active, affirmative, declarative sentence used as an example only approximates the base structure. Rules such as these are referred to as rules of transformation and a grammar that contains such rules as a transformational grammar.

The important point to be made here is that language symbols cannot be used arbitrarily but must follow the rules of the grammar of the language, and these rules exist on all levels of language usage. The structure and function of these rules will be clarified and some specific examples given in the discussion of "Experiments in Psycholinguistics."

A second fact about language is that it consists of at least two levels: a surface structure level and a deep structure level. Consider, for example, the following sentences:

1. John is easy to please.

2. John is eager to please.

On the surface these sentences appear very much alike in structure. If we diagrammed these sentences, both would be given the same diagram. Their differences, however, are brought out when we attempt to apply various transformations to them. We can say, for example, "It is easy to please John" without changing the meaning of the sentence. However, when we apply the exact same operation to 2.), there is a drastic change—"It is eager to please John." In 1.) John is the object of the action; it is John who is pleased by someone else. But in 2.) John is the subject of the action; it is John who performs the act of pleasing. Note also that the adjective *eager* modifies John in 2.) but that *easy* in 1.) modifies not John but the sentence as a whole.

Of course, many examples could be used to illustrate that sentences that appear alike on the surface are actually quite different when analyzed more completely. Since sentences may be alike in surface structure and yet differ in significant ways, another level of language is postulated—a level of deep structure. The importance and, in fact, the existence of deep structure is probably most obvious when we attempt to deal with ambiguity. Consider, for example, sentence 3.).

3. They were rewarded by the machine.

This sentence is ambiguous in at least two ways. It may mean that they were rewarded near the machine or that the machine rewarded them. The surface structure of this sentence, however, gives no clue to its ambiguity. We cannot diagram this sentence in different ways in order to illustrate its two meanings. Because of this, the existence of deep structure is inferred. In generative-transformational grammar (Chomsky 1965, 1968) all sentences are viewed as having at least one deep structure, ambiguous sentences as having at least two deep structures. Sentence 3.) would have deep structures resembling 4.) and 5.).

4. They were rewarded near the machine.

5. The machine rewarded them.

The last point that needs to be made is the distinction between competence and performance. Competence is viewed as the native speaker's knowledge of his language; it is his knowledge of the rules or grammar of language. Performance, on the other hand, is the actual concrete manifestations or realizations of these rules; it is the actual speech and the understanding of speech. The importance of this distinction is great. Competence is not identical to performance, nor is there a one-to-one or isomorphic relationship between the two. Performance is influenced by numerous extra-linguistic factors such as memory span, attention, motivation, fatigue, and the like. Competence is uninfluenced by such psychological factors; it is linguistic knowledge untouched by human limitations. Competence, to use an analogy cited by Katz and Postal (1964, p. ix), is like a symphony in the abstract; performance is like the symphony as performed and heard. Only in an idealized orchestra and audience would the symphony and the symphony-as-played-and-heard be identical. Similarly, only in an idealized speaker and listener would linguistic competence and performance be identical.

A grammar of a language may then be viewed as a device for generating or describing all the grammatical sentences and none of the ungrammatical sentences of the language. It is a device that describes the competence which native speakers of that language have. A language, therefore, may be defined as that set of infinite sentences that the grammar generates.

**Psychological theory**   It should be clear that a theory of language is not the same as a theory of a language user. A theory of language is an abstract characterization of the facts of language. The task of psychology and of psycholinguistics in particular is to construct, on the basis of the facts of language contained in the linguistic theory, a model of language performance, a model of how the linguistic competence is utilized. Such a theory or model can only be constructed from complete and accurate data about language. In reality, however, the data on language are far from complete and probably in many respects inaccurate. Yet, the psycholinguist assumes that the language data provided by linguistics are, in basic outline at least, accurate and that whatever else is added to the linguistic description of a language or of language in general will not drastically alter what has already been presented. It is on this basis that a performance model is created.

At the time of this writing, mid-1971, there is no psychological theory that is completely compatible with the linguistic facts. No current theory adequately explains language behavior as it is described by linguists. There have, however, been a number of important theories constructed, which explain at least in part some of the mechanisms that may govern or describe language behavior.

One of the best-known attempts to construct a model of verbal behavior is that of B. F. Skinner (1957), perhaps most famous for his contributions to teaching machines and programmed learning. To Skinner, verbal behavior is operant behavior; it is emitted by an organism without observable or identifiable stimuli and is maintained by reinforcement. Put differently, verbal behavior, to Skinner, is controlled by its consequences or contingencies. When its consequences are rewarding, the behavior is maintained and is increased in frequency and strength; when its consequences are punishing, the behavior decreases in frequency and strength or is extinguished.

The goal of Skinner's theory is two-fold (Skinner 1957, p. 10):

Our first responsibility is simple *description:* what is the topography of this subdivision of human behavior? Once that question has been answered in at least a preliminary fashion, we may advance to the stage called *explanation:* what conditions are relevant to the occurrence of the behavior—what are the variables of which it is a function? Once these have been identified, we can account for the dynamic characteristics of verbal behavior within a framework appropriate to human behavior as a whole. At the same time, of course, we must consider the behavior of the listener. In relating this to the behavior of the speaker, we complete our account of the verbal episode.

Skinner's "theory" thus takes the form of a listing of verbal operants and of the conditions under which they are controlled.

The *mand* is a verbal operant which comes under the control of a particular drive state. For example, a thirsty man will call for "water" and a hungry child for "milk." These mands specify the behavior of the listener, which is required to reduce the drive state, the actual reinforcement, or both.

The *tact* is a labeling response under the control of stimuli from physical objects. When a person sees a pen and says "pen," he is engaging in tacting behavior.

*Echoic* behavior is controlled by previously heard speech and partially or totally duplicates it. Partially echoic behavior is seen in the tendency to respond in word association tests with clang associates, that is, responses that are phonetically similar to the stimulus word. In its extreme and pathological form it is seen as echolalia where the individual repeats everything he hears.

*Textual* behavior is controlled by nonauditory verbal stimuli, the most common of which are orthographic symbols. A "text," however, may also consist of pictographs, phonetic symbols, or any other nonauditory verbal stimuli. When a speaker says [θɪŋ] in response to the written symbols "thing," he is engaging in textual behavior.

*Intraverbal* behavior is controlled by other verbal behavior with which it is closely associated but from which it differs in form. Intraverbal behavior is most often seen in completion responses. Upon hearing "Forescore and" we engage in intraverbal behavior when we complete this and say "seven years ago." Many of the responses on word association tests are of this type of behavior.

Verbal behavior may also be controlled by the *audience* variable as when, for example, the child sees his mother and says "candy." The audience, of course, also influences the topic or content of verbal behavior as well as its form or style. We do not speak about the same things or in the same way to widely differing audiences.

When verbal behavior is reinforced, its frequency, according to Skinner, increases; when it is punished, it decreases in frequency. For example, if an individual demanded "water" and water was given to him, his verbal behavior would be said to be positively reinforced. If his verbal behavior resulted in the termination of an aversive stimulus, for example the shutting off of an uncomfortable sound, he would be negatively reinforced. In both cases the reinforcement results in strengthening the verbal operants. On future similar occasions the probability of these verbal operants being emitted is greatly increased. On the other hand, if the individual were punished, say he was slapped for asking too many questions, this verbal behavior would decrease in frequency and possibly become extinguished.

Skinner's *Verbal Behavior*, then, is simply a logical extension of his views on operant conditioning as applied to behavior generally, an approach that has much to recommend it for anyone concerned with modifying or changing behavior (see, for example, Sloane and MacAulay 1968 and DeVito 1969a).

The most obvious problem with such a conception of language behavior is that there is no place in the theory for meaning. Psychological processes dependent upon or influenced by meaning can, therefore, not be explained or even described. For example, with frequent repetition words lose some of their meaning as measured, say, on the semantic differential.[4] This phenomenon of semantic satiation cannot, however, be explained by a theory that has no mechanism for dealing with meaning. Similarly, semantic generalization—the phenomenon by which behavioral responses gen-

---

[4] Briefly, the semantic differential is a device for measuring the connotative meaning of concepts and consists of seven-point scales bound by polar opposites, e.g., good-bad, strong-weak, hot-cold. Meaning is viewed as consisting of evaluative, potency, and activity dimensions. See Osgood, Suci, and Tannenbaum (1957) for the original development of this instrument and Snider and Osgood (1969) for discussions of the validity and reliability of the semantic differential and for a collection of research studies utilizing this measuring instrument. Darnell (1970) provides an excellent discussion of the theory of semantic differentiation and suggests numerous applications of this instrument to communication research.

eralize on a meaning basis, as, for example, among synonyms—cannot be explained.[5]

Another difficulty facing this theory is to account for the fact that sentences—with only trivial exceptions—are novel utterances. They are created by the speaker and must be processed by the hearer as novel stimuli. This fact of language poses a serious problem for a theory based on conditioning. Put simply, how can a theory that deals with behavior in terms of stimulus-response bonds handle language behavior, which is almost always novel?

Because of such "inadequacies" other psychologists have attempted to broaden the base of the theory and thus explain more of the relevant linguistic data. Most notable among these attempts are those of O. Hobart Mowrer (1960) and Charles E. Osgood (1963a, b, 1968). In simplified form, these theories hold that a word is learned or gets its meaning from direct or indirect association with the object or referent. After repeated pairings, the word comes to elicit a mediating response, which is part of the response that would normally be made to the actual object. The response to the word "fire," for example, is held to be part of the response that would normally be made to the referent, that is, the actual fire.

According to Mowrer, the sentence is essentially a conditioning device; the copula verb functions to associate the predicate with the subject. The sentence "Tom is a thief," to use Mowrer's example, is understood because the response to "thief" transfers to "Tom," and on future occasions we respond to "Tom" as we had previously responded to "thief." Mediational theories such as those of Mowrer and Osgood are actually much more complex than this would indicate, but this seems the essential pattern.

Mediational theories account rather directly for meaning by postulating that the linguistic stimulus elicits a mediating response that is self-stimulating, and this self-stimulation then leads to what Osgood calls a representational mediation process, which is meaning. In semantic satiation this process is temporarily inhibited. Semantic generalization is considered the consequence of a process by which synonymous words set off similar or identical representational mediating processes, which naturally lead to the same or similar overt behavior.

[5] Skinner's theory has come under attack from a number of different points of view. Morris (1958) has criticized it from a philosophical and Osgood (1958) from a psychological perspective. Both reviewers find its major fault to be its failure to deal with meaning and conclude that the model is therefore insufficient and incomplete. The most thorough criticism has come from Chomsky (1959) who concludes that the model is not incomplete but incorrect.

These theories, however, leave a number of questions unanswered when they attempt to deal with sentences.[6] As already noted, all sentences have deep structures that influence various psychological processes and hence have psychological reality. Yet, deep structure is never made overt; no one speaks in deep structures. And, as many linguists have pointed out, a theory that deals solely with stimuli and responses can only deal with linguistic facts that are overt, i.e., that exist in the surface structure. Consequently, they cannot deal with deep structures, which are never overt but which nevertheless are psychologically real.

Mediational theories attempt to explain the learning and understanding of different types of words with the same basic processes. In the sentence "Tom is a thief" the learning and understanding of both "Tom" and "thief" are accounted for in essentially the same way. Yet, as Fodor (1965) has demonstrated, they function quite differently. Notice that one can say "Who is Tom?" but not "Who is thief?" One can say "What is a thief?" but not "What is a Tom?" These words, then, are treated differently in the language, and a theory of language behavior must account for these differences. Berlyne (1966, p. 410), however, has argued: "It is not conceivable that names and predicates might be different with respect to the wording of the questions by which we inquire into their meaning and yet similar in other respects, including those with which Mowrer is concerned?" While this is certainly true, a viable theory cannot be built around only certain facts of language while ignoring others. If it is to deal with language, then it must deal with all of its complexities.

Another criticism of mediational theories is that these theories do not deal effectively with the question of belief. The theories hold that responses will transfer from the predicate to the subject, as in the example "Tom is a thief." Yet, intuitively we know that such responses will not transfer when we do not believe the sentence. Similarly, we will not respond to the word "fire" in the same way as to the actual fire unless we believe that there is a fire present. Our understanding of these sentences, of course, is independent of our belief or disbelief. Exactly how these theories will incorporate a mechanism for dealing with belief is not clear.

Modifications and improvements in these theories may, in the future, render them more satisfactory than they are at present for dealing with language behavior. Of course, it is also possible that they will prove to

[6] For a provocative exchange of views on the adequacy-inadequacy of mediational theory see Fodor's (1965) criticism, Osgood's (1966) and Berlyne's (1966) defense, and Fodor's (1966) rebuttal. Also see Osgood's (1968) attempt to bridge the gap between linguistic and behavior theory.

be in principle inadequate to the task (cf. Bever, 1968). The theories of Skinner, Mowrer, and Osgood, although not complete explications of language behavior, nevertheless offer significant insights into this most complex of human behaviors.

Clearly, we seem far from realizing an adequate model of language performance. The summary statement of Miller and McNeill (1969, p. 688) seems appropriate here.

In summary, the most we can say concerning a grammatical performance model is that it must incorporate a component that represents the language user's grammatical competence; that it must process speech in a single pass from left to right, in real time; that it is constrained by the limitations of short-term memory; that it must allow for both the production and the reception of speech; and that it can be generalized to ungrammatical materials. A great diversity of models might be constructed within these broad boundaries; it is one of the tasks of experimental psycholinguists to collect evidence that will narrow these boundaries until they converge on a satisfactory model of performance.

## Experiments in psycholinguistics

There has been so much experimental research in psycholinguistics in the last twenty years that any attempt to review it will almost surely be incomplete and will certainly be dated in only a few months. Yet, since this literature is essential to an understanding of psycholinguistics as a whole, it is necessary that some attempt be made to discuss it even within these obvious limitations.

Beginning with the smallest units and working up to the largest, this section considers research in hesitation phenomena, phonology, semantics, syntax, style, and language-as-a-whole. The purpose of this section is to characterize rather than survey the literature, and to this end examples rather than reviews are given. Hopefully, these few examples will provide some insight into the nature and function of psycholinguistic research and will, most importantly, stimulate the asking of relevant and meaningful questions.

**Hesitation phenomena**  Before the advent of psycholinguistics, research in speech and language concentrated almost exclusively on the verbal dimension, i.e., on the sounds, words, and sentences used by speakers. Those few researchers who investigated the nonverbal aspects such as pausing, nonfluencies, and various other hesitation types were concerned primarily with defective speech as in, for example, stuttering. However, in the past few decades or so a great deal of research has been directed to the investigation of hesitation phenomena in normally "fluent" speakers. This word "fluent" is perhaps misleading. One of the interesting facts that emerges from this research is that speech, although referred to by such phrases as "spout," "stream," and "torrent", all denoting fluency and unbroken continuity, is interrupted to a significant degree by hesitations. For example, in spontaneous speech 50% of speech is broken up by hesitations into units of less than three words, 75% into units of less than five words, and 90% into units of less than ten words. A similar picture emerges when the time taken for pauses is calculated. For example, in interview situations 4% to 54% of the speakers' time was taken up by pauses. In discussion situations the pause time was even greater; between 13% and 63% of the time was taken up by pauses. In spontaneous speech 16% to 62% of utterance time was taken up by silence. "These values," says Goldman-Eisler (1968, p. 18), from whose research the above figures were taken, "seem to be ample evidence that pausing is as much part of speech as vocal utterance."

Research in hesitation phenomena has been addressed to numerous and diverse questions. Researchers have attempted to correlate hesitations with units of linguistic structure (Lounsbury 1965; Maclay and Osgood 1959; Blankenship and Kay 1964), to find points of contact between hesitation phenomena and thinking processes (Goldman-Eisler 1968), to infer various psychological states (Mahl 1956), to examine the influence these hesitations have on listeners (McCroskey and Mehrley 1969) and conversely to examine the influence that listeners have on hesitations (Fleshler 1969), and, of course, to examine the implications of hesitations for stuttering, its analysis and etiology (DeVito, 1970a, pp. 169–184).

Hesitations may be classified in various different ways depending upon the specific needs and interests of the researcher. One classification, proposed by Maclay and Osgood (1959, p. 24), may be used to illustrate the diversity of hesitation types:

1. Repeats
   1.1 of one or more lexical items
   1.2 of less than one lexical item

2. False Starts
   2.1 involving sentence correction, i.e., where the grammatical pattern of the sentence is changed

2.2 involving a word correction, where the word changed is of the same part of speech as the corrected word

3. Filled Pauses, containing such hesitation markers as [ɛ], [m], and [ə]

4. Unfilled Pauses
   4.1 involving silence of unusual length
   4.2 involving the nonphonemic lengthening of phonemes

If one were concerned with hesitation phenomena in reading, additional classifications would be necessary, for example:

5. Change in Word Order

6. Word Change

7. Omissions
   7.1 of one or more lexical items
   7.2 of less than one lexical item

8. Additions
   8.1 of one or more lexical items
   8.2 of less than one lexical item

9. Sentence Structure Change

A few examples of research in hesitation phenomena may further characterize this area of research. Floyd Lounsbury (1965) advanced the hypothesis that hesitation phenomena correspond to the points of high uncertainty in linguistic units of any size. That is, persons will hesitate most often at those points at which the language allows for the greatest number of choices. Thus, for example, in a normal sentence most hesitations would occur before content words rather than function words, before initial words of phrases or clauses than before medial or final words, and so on. This hypothesis has been substantiated by the research of Maclay and Osgood (1959) and Goldman-Eisler (1968).

Another hypothesis is that hesitations are correlated with the various psychological states of the organism. Lerea (1956), for example, found that nonfluencies were significantly related to an individual's degree of nervousness, and Mahl (1956) found that silences were significantly longer in high anxious phases of interviews than in low anxious phases.

Hesitations have also been related to various cognitive processes. For example, Goldman-Eisler (1968) found that pausing time was approximately twice as great when Ss interpreted meaning than when they simply described content.

Still another hypothesis might be formulated around listeners' reactions, specifically that hesitations both influence and are influenced by audience responses. McCroskey and Mehrley (1969), for example, found that extensive nonfluencies significantly reduced the amount of attitude change produced by the speaker. And Fleshler (1969) found, contrary to the commonsense assumption of Stolz and Tannenbaum (1963) who suggested that a favorable audience response will lead to reduced nonfluencies, that speakers had significantly fewer nonfluencies when addressing an inattentive audience than when addressing an attentive audience.

To the extent that research on hesitation phenomena has implications for the way in which speech is produced and understood, it is directly significant for a theory of psycholinguistics and indirectly for any science of speech and language behavior. For the student of communicative disorders the study of hesitation phenomena has direct relevance for stuttering which is, to my way of thinking, nothing more than extreme hesitations. When hesitations become extreme, various behavioral modifications are introduced (facial contortions, hand pounding, and the like) and to these hesitations so compounded the word "stuttering" is applied.

**Phonology**   Native speakers of English feel intuitively that certain combinations of sounds are somehow "right" or are "English-like" whereas other combinations sound "strange," "foreign," or "unlike-English." Most native speakers, for example, would agree that STRIK, although not an English word, is nevertheless "like English" and could logically be an English word. STWAP, on the other hand, sounds foreign or strange; no English word makes use of the consonant cluster STW. Yet, it does not sound as strange or as foreign as KVSPL, for example.

Probably, native speakers of English have somehow internalized a rule for permissible and nonpermissible phoneme combinations, which accounts for the great agreement among native speakers as to the "Englishness" or "non-Englishness" of various sound combinations. The linguist has attempted to phrase this rule as simply and as economically as possible. Benjamin Lee Whorf (Carroll, 1956, p. 223), for example, expressed the rule as in Figure 1.

With this rule we can construct sequences of phonemes that would be permissible in English as well as sequences that violate the formula in varying degrees; for example, sequences that contain only one violation, sequences that contain two violations, and so on. From this we may derive a list of "words" ranging all the way from completely like English to completely unlike English.

Using the above intuitions and linguistic description, Greenberg and

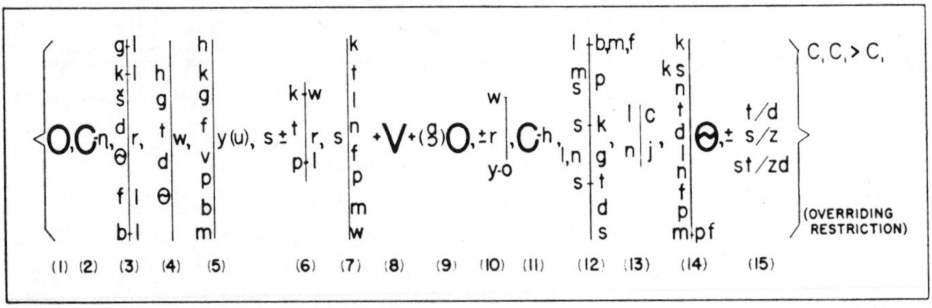

**Figure 1** *Structural formula of the monosyllabic word in English (standard midwestern American). The formula can be simplified by special symbols for certain groups of letters, but this simplification would make it harder to explain. The simplest possible formula for a monosyllabic word is C + V, and some languages actually conform to this. Polynesian has the next most simple formula, O, C + V.*

Jenkins (1964) attempted to investigate some of the psychological correlates of phoneme sequences. Words were composed that varied in degree of closeness to English. Each word was assigned a numerical value, which indicated the degree to which it varied from normal English. These words were read to a group of college students. Three different research approaches were tried. In the free magnitude estimation approach the Ss were instructed to select a number for the first word they heard. The number could be large or small; it was simply used as a base. As a response to the second word they were to select a number that reflected the degree to which the second word differed from the first. For example, if a S gave the number 100 to the first word and if the second word was felt to be twice as far from English as the first, he would give to it a number twice as large, i.e., 200. If the second word was much more similar to English than the first, he would give it a smaller number, say 40 or 50 or 60. The correlation between these estimates and the linguistic scale that measured the degree to which the words deviated from the rule was .94, which is highly significant.

In the second method the students rated the words on an eleven point scale, ranging from very like English to very unlike English. Here again the ratings correlated very highly (.95) with the linguistic scale measurements.

In the third method the Ss were instructed to write down as many associations as they could think of for each word they heard. The results here indicated that for those words that were very close to English the

Ss recorded the greatest number of associations, with the number of associations decreasing as the words became more unlike English.

Smith and Koutstaal (1969) had Ss listen to these same words and attend to the tongue, lips, and jaw movements involved in subvocalizing these sounds. They were then instructed to rate these words on a nine point scale in terms of the effort required to pronounce them. These ratings of effort correlated .79 with the linguistic scale values of Greenberg and Jenkins, indicating that Ss perceived unlike-English words to require much effort and like-English words to require little effort.

In another study utilizing this same formula for phoneme combination, Stanley Messer (1967) found that even children between the ages of 3.1 and 4.5 could distinguish words that were constructed in accordance with the formula from those that violated the formula.

Apparently this formula, which appears so complex, is learned by the child at a very early age with no apparent difficulty and with no explicit teaching. How the child does this is a question that developmental psycholinguistics must confront.

Another approach to the investigation of phonology concentrates on the relationship between sound and meaning or, as it has come to be called, phonetic symbolism. In a classic study Edward Sapir (1929) had Ss match nonsense syllables with objects. For example, *mil* and *mal* were presented to the Ss who were told that one was the name for a large table and one for a small table. Which was which? About 80% of the Ss agreed that *mil* stood for the small table and *mal* for the large one. Since the consonants were the same in both words, the differences in perceived magnitude must have been due to the vowels. Of course, many other similar examples were used before any conclusions were drawn. Stanley Newman (1933) later analyzed Sapir's data and found that the tested vowels could be arranged in order of perceived magnitude from small to large as follows: /i, e, ɛ, æ, and a/. This ordering is particularly significant since it duplicates the receding positions of articulation made by the tongue in the mouth, the decreasing frequencies of vocal resonance, and the increasing size of the oral cavity used in pronunciation. This, and similar findings, led to the hypothesis that phonetic symbolism is a universal of language and more specifically that these magnitude relationships would hold for all languages. That is, since these sounds are produced the same way by all persons regardless of the specific language they speak, all persons would perceive these sounds in the same way. A number of cross-linguistic investigations of phonetic symbolism were thus initiated in an attempt to test this hypothesis of universality. Other sounds and other semantic dimensions (e.g., strong-weak, pleasant-unpleasant) were added by other researchers, but the results are still inconclusive (e.g., Miron 1961; Taylor and Taylor 1962).

Because of the failure to find universal phonetic symbolism, other investigators postulated that the sound-meaning relationships found in individual languages were due to the feedback from the existing words in the language. Thus, /a/ was perceived as larger than /i/ not because it was made in a different manner but rather because it appeared in more words denoting largeness in that language whereas /i/ appeared in more words denoting smallness (cf. Taylor and Taylor, 1965).

So far neither the phonetic placement theory nor the feedback theory is conclusively supported. It will probably turn out that both theories are correct, but only in part. That is, the perceived relationships between sound and meaning are probably due to both the manner of articulation and the frequencies with which certain sounds denoting specific meanings appear in a language.

Still another major research thrust in the area of phonology concerns speech perception, particularly the relationship between phonetic interpretation and the actual acoustic properties of the sound. Since the work on speech perception is reviewed elsewhere in this series, it will suffice here to merely point out the problem that such research findings pose for psycholinguistics and for any theory of language behavior. Segments that differ on a purely acoustic basis, when surrounded by different phonemes, are perceived as identical. Similarly, certain segments of identical acoustic properties, when surrounded by different phonemes, are perceived differently. For example, Bever (1968, p. 490) points out that "the acoustic structure of the 't' in 'stew' is identical with that of the 'k' in 'ski,' yet they are perceived as phonetically distinct. This kind of finding (largely due to Haskins Laboratory) is particularly important since the phonetic-acoustic level appeared to be the last reasonable hope for the application of behaviorist principles to the structure of language." Although much further research and replication is needed in this area, it appears from the available findings that current learning theories are far from the stage when they can convincingly explain such perceptual phenomena.

**Semantics**   Relatively few psycholinguistic studies have been conducted in the area of semantics, though it should be obvious that meaning is the single most important aspect of language. Nevertheless, the area of semantics has been neglected to a considerable extent, due in no small way to the failure of linguistics to provide a clear and coherent framework for semantic analysis (though see, for example, Jakobovits and Miron 1967, pp. 355-636).

Fortunately, amid this sparcity is one of the most insightful and provocative psycholinguistic hypotheses—the Pollyanna hypothesis, developed by Jerry Boucher and Charles E. Osgood (1969). The Pollyanna hypothesis states "that there is a universal human tendency to use evaluatively positive (E+) words more frequently, diversely, and facilely than evaluatively negative (E−) words" (Boucher and Osgood 1969, p. 1).

In order to test the validity of this hypothesis a number of specific analyses were conducted. One such analysis concerned the responses of 100 high school boys in 13 different languages to 100 culture common words. The Ss were simply asked to supply the first qualifier that occurred to them for each of the 100 words. The results showed that E+ qualifiers were given more often and were used with more different stimulus words than were the E− words.

Another analysis centered on the application of negative affixes in different languages. In English a positive word (e.g., *happy*) can be made negative by applying a negative affix (e.g., *unhappy*). Similarly, a negative word (e.g., *broken*) can be made positive by applying a negative affix (e.g., *unbroken*). The question relevant to the Pollyanna hypothesis is which pattern is more common in the various languages of the world. The hypothesis assumes that the usual pattern is for the negative affix to be joined to an initially positive word to form a negatively evaluated word. The hypothesis assumes, in other words, the priority of positively evaluated terms in the historical development of any language. Additional words are then added by applying negative affixes to already existing terms. In all 11 languages analyzed this predicted pattern was found.

Another prediction of the hypothesis is that in the development of the child E+ words will be acquired before E− words. This prediction is also supported. E+ words are always more frequent than E− words in human language, with the difference between them greatest in the early years of the child and declining with age.

The most provocative part of this hypothesis is the reason for the Pollyanna effect. That is, why are positively evaluated words used more frequently, diversely, and facilely than negatively evaluated words? One explanation, advanced by Robert Zajonc (1968), is that mere exposure to stimuli generates positive attitude or evaluation. We like best the person we are around most, we agree with the positions we hear most often, we like to do the things we do most often, and so on. The alternative explanation, of course, is that positive evaluation leads to high frequency rather than the other way around. Boucher and Osgood (1969) argue that positively evaluated words do not become so because of exposure but rather they are used frequently because they are positive. Thus, while both explanations agree that positive evaluation and frequency go together, they differ on the causal relationship accounting for the correlation.

Rather than attempt to argue for one of these explanations, the conclusion of Boucher and Osgood (1969, p. 8) is more appropriate:

We are left with the question of why E+ words should tend to be used more frequently by humans than E− words. Why do most people most of the time in most places around the world talk about the good things in life? Why do they tend to see and report the good qualities of things? The answer surely goes beyond psycholinguistics *per se* and into the nature of human social structures and the conditions under which these structures can be maintained. It is hard to imagine human groups whose members persistently look for and talk about the ugly things in life and in their neighbors long remaining together. We leave further elaboration to social philosophers.

**Syntax**  It is in the area of syntax where most of the psycholinguistic studies have been conducted. Here there are two principal research trends. One focus is to analyze the various different sentence types in terms of their psychological correlates.

For a theory of human communication, especially for one concerned with communicative effectiveness, one important dimension is the relative ease of understanding various sentence types. In one study, for example, the relative ease of recalling and understanding active as opposed to passive sentences was analyzed (DeVito, 1969b). After hearing all test sentences once and then being provided with the initial noun phrase as a prompt, Ss were asked to recall the entire sentence. Regardless of how the reproductions were scored (e.g., number of verb phrases correct, number of noun phrases correct, number of complete sentences correct) the active sentences proved easier to recall. Understanding was measured by cloze procedure.[7] Active and passive passages were constructed and mutilated by deleting every fifth word. Ss were then instructed to fill in the words

---

[7] Briefly, cloze procedure is a method for measuring the difficulty and the listener's/reader's comprehension of a message. In the usual procedure a passage is mutilated by deleting every fifth word. The receivers must then fill in the omitted words from the context which remains. One point is scored for each correct fill-in. See Taylor (1953, 1956) and DeVito (1967a).

they felt to be missing. The passive passage proved easier to understand when verbatim fill-ins were scored as correct, but the active version proved easier when fill-ins of the same part of speech as the omitted word were scored correct.

In a study just completed (DeVito 1970b) 108 yes/no questions were composed representing nine different transformations (e.g., Does the circle follow the square? The circle doesn't follow the square, does it?). Each question was keyed to a diagram and the Ss were instructed to simply look at the diagram and answer the questions presented on a speeded-up tape. The number of errors constituted the measure of difficulty for each question type. The results demonstrated that active questions are easier than passives, affirmatives easier than negatives, nontags easier than tags (e.g., a sentence containing "doesn't it" or "isn't it" tagged to the end), and neutrals easier than loaded (i.e., a question which specifies the answer the questioner is seeking).

There are, of course, many similar studies, which might be cited along these same lines (cf. Miller 1962; Garrett and Fodor 1968). These studies are important in developing scientifically verifiable principles of communication but are of less interest to the development of psycholinguistic theory than those conducted as examinations of the psychological reality of linguistic constructs. This second research approach may be illustrated with two cleverly designed experiments.

In one, conducted by Blumenthal and Boakes (1967), the notion of deep and surface structure was examined. Of the twenty sentences used, ten were similar in form to 6.) and ten were similar in form to 7.).

6. John is eager to please.

7. John is easy to please.

As already noted, in 6.) *John* is the logical subject of the sentence and in 7.) *John* is the logical object. Further, in 6.) the adjective *eager* modifies *John* whereas in 7.) *easy* modifies the entire sentence.

The experimenters presented Ss with the sentences and asked them to recall them. Some Ss were given the initial noun phrase and others the adjective as prompts. The initial noun phrase facilitated recall of type 6.) more than type 7.) sentences, whereas the adjective facilitated recall of type 7.) better than type 6.) sentences.

The important point made by this study is that differences in deep structure—the only difference between these sentence types—must have accounted for the differences in recall ability and thus that deep structure is psychologically real.

Another study in a similar vein was conducted by Garrett, Bever, and Fodor (1966). These researchers used sentences of types 8.) and 9.).

8.   In her *hope of marrying Anna was surely impractical.*

9.   Your *hope of marrying Anna was surely impractical.*

These sentences were then recorded on a parallel tape and clicks inserted at nine places on each tape. Note that the italicized portions of the sentences are identical; the prefatory words, however, change the structure of these "identical" parts. We would normally divide sentence 8.) between *marrying* and *Anna,* but the division in 9.) would be between *Anna* and *was.* The Ss were presented with sentences of these types and simply asked to write down the sentences and indicate where they heard the click. The results clearly demonstrated that the perception of the clicks (regardless of where they objectively occurred on the tape) was toward the syntactic breaks. That is, the Ss moved the clicks toward the syntactic break. They perceived the clicks as coinciding or being closer to the syntactic break than was the case objectively. Like the previous study, this one demonstrates the psychological reality of syntactic structure.

Other studies have focused on somewhat different aspects of syntax. Savin and Perchonock (1965), for example, had Ss recall sentences of different transformational complexities along with a series of unrelated words. It was found that when sentences involved a number of transformations (e.g., passive negatives, passive questions), fewer of the unrelated words were recalled than when the sentences involved few transformations (e.g., simple questions, simple passives). The authors reason that the sentences that involve a number of transformations occupy more memory space and consequently less is available for the unrelated words. And Gough (1965, 1966) found that verification time was less for active than for passive, for affirmative than for negative, and for true than for false sentences.

These findings, and many others on syntax which might have been cited, illustrate that syntactic structure is not merely some abstract creation of the linguist but rather that it has a psychological reality; it influences such psychological processes as comprehension, memory, and perception.[8]

**Style**   The next level of language analysis, considered by many linguists

[8] The studies mentioned here have been derived from the generative transformational linguistic theory proposed by Chomsky. A number of other studies, however, have been based on the depth hypothesis developed by Yngve (1960). See, for example, Miller and McNeill (1969).

to be outside the domain of linguistics proper but of considerable importance to any theory of psycholinguistics, is that of stylistic analysis.

Style may be defined as the selection and arrangement of those linguistic features that are open to choice. In other words, style begins where grammar leaves off. As the rules of grammar fail to apply, the stylistic freedom increases (DeVito 1967c).

Roman Jakobson (1960) has proposed that as the linguistic units get larger in size, say from phonemes to morphemes, to words, to phrases, to sentences, the freedom of choice increases and hence the opportunity for stylistic variation. For example, in the sentence frame "The ____ is good" there is considerable choice. Any noun-word can be placed in the frame. But there is not complete freedom; a verb or an adjective, for example, could not be used. Grammar dictates that a noun-word be used, but the particular noun-word chosen is a matter of style. In the frame "The boy ____" we can see that there is considerably more freedom of choice than in the previous frame. Into this frame one could fit a verb phrase, a nominative phrase, another noun, a conjunction, and so on. The freedom is almost unlimited.

Approaching style as a psycholinguistic problem, we attempt to analyze the language in an effort to make inferences about the source producing the message. The assumption made here is that stylistic variation is a function of the psychological state of the organism encoding; when these psychological states vary, so does the style of his messages. The task of stylistic analysis in a psycholinguistic context has been succinctly expressed by Fillmore Sanford (1942, p. 197) long before the field of psycholinguistics even had a name.

From what we know of personality we might well expect that the individual's verbal and nonverbal behaviors are all of a piece and that we can, if we are clever, see the latter in the former. Studies of style are likely to have psychodiagnostic value. Linguistic traits, however, quite aside from the light they may throw on nonlinguistic behavior, are in themselves important data. The most frequent and most consummately human of human behaviors is speech. When we have characterized the person's speech we have gone a long way toward characterizing the person.

Since thorough reviews of this "psychostylistics" literature are readily available (Mahl and Schulze 1964; Nunnally 1965) we may single out just one study to illustrate this general strategy.[9]

Probably the best-known study in this area was conducted by Osgood

[9] For excellent reviews of research strategies for the analysis of message content see Bowers (1970), and for message style see Lynch (1970).

and Walker (1959). These researchers analyzed suicide notes produced by actual suicide victims and compared these with ordinary letters written by others to friends and relatives. On the basis of motivational theory the authors formulated four hypotheses. When compared with ordinary letters, suicide notes would be characterized by 1.) greater stereotypy since increased motivational drive would lead to the use of those lexical and syntactic alternatives that were most familiar and habitual; 2.) greater number of lexical and syntactic choices related to the motives leading to self-destruction; 3.) greater conflict and compromise since suicide would logically involve competing motives; and 4.) greater disorganization since extreme increases in drive state would probably lead to disruptions in those behaviors that require fine coordination such as encoding a message.

Suicide notes were found to display greater stereotypy. Suicide notes contained shorter, simpler, and less diverse vocabulary; the writing was more repetitious, contained more allness terms, and was more predictable, as measured by cloze procedure. The second hypothesis was also supported; suicide notes did contain more linguistic elements associated with self-destruction, e.g., more distress-expressing phrases, less terms which were positively evaluated, and more mands. The third hypothesis, too, was supported; suicide notes revealed greater evidence of conflict. Verb phrases, for example, were qualified more often, and there were significantly more evaluative assertions referring to the writer himself or to those who were close to him, which were ambivalent in sign, i.e., positive or negative. The last hypothesis was not supported; suicide notes did not reveal more structural disturbances.

Osgood and Walker also asked students to assume the state of a suicide victim and write suicide notes. When analyzed, these notes were found to contain many of the elements of the actual suicide notes but did not contain the demanding tone, the reduced qualification, or the evaluative ambivalence of the genuine suicide notes. It appears that although persons can assume the state of a suicide victim, at least to some extent, there are significant differences, which are revealed in the messages of the two groups.

It may be hypothesized—along with Ben Jonson—that "language most showeth a man." Admittedly, however, it is extremely difficult to determine how and in what way such connections manifest themselves. Nevertheless, it seems legitimate to assume that such connections do exist, and it remains for future research to specify them, however subtle and elusive they may be.

**Language and languages** The highest or largest unit with which the psycholinguist deals is obviously the language itself, and here he may be interested in comparing different languages in terms of the psychological correlates or in comparing different dialects or codes of a given language or perhaps in describing the universals or features common to all languages. Each of these three approaches may be illustrated briefly.

The comparison of different languages in terms of the psychological concomitants goes under many different names, the Sapir-Whorf Hypothesis, the Whorfian Thesis, the Sapir-Whorf-Korzybski Hypothesis, the Linguistic Weltanschauung Thesis, and probably numerous others. The basic assumption of these theses is that the language one speaks influences his thought and behavior. The most extreme statement of this position was probably given by Benjamin Lee Whorf (Carroll 1956, pp. 212–213).

. . . the background linguistic system (in other words, the grammar) of each language is not merely a reproducing instrument for voicing ideas but rather is itself the shaper of ideas, the program and guide for the individual's mental activity, for his analysis of impressions, for his synthesis of his mental stock in trade. . . . We dissect nature along lines laid down by our native languages. The categories and types that we isolate from the world of phenomena we do not find there because they stare every observer in the face; on the contrary the world is presented in a kaleidoscopic flux of impressions which has to be organized by our minds—and this means largely by the linguistic systems of our minds.

If Whorf is correct, then it should follow that we will react differently to those categories that our language treats differently than do other languages and also that persons speaking widely differing languages will react in different ways to the same phenomena. Brown and Lenneberg (1954) studied Ss responses to colors. They predicted that when a color has a short name (high codability), Ss will respond quickly, be in close agreement with one another on the name, and agree with themselves from one trial to another. Conversely, when a color has a longer name, Ss, when asked to name it, would respond more slowly, show more disagreement among each other, and show disagreement with themselves from one trial to another.

Ss were shown 24 colors and were asked to name each as quickly as possible. Five Ss were then recalled after one month and put through the same procedure again. From their responses four measures were taken: the length of the naming response in syllables, the average reaction time, the degree of agreement among Ss, and the degree of agreement between

Ss for those tested twice. All three hypotheses were supported; the average reaction time increased with the length of the name and the degree of agreement among and between Ss varied inversely with the length of the name.

These experimenters went a step further and attempted to relate these initial findings to behavioral correlates. For this test 120 colors were mounted on a large white board. Four colors (for which codability scores were already available from the previous experiment) were then exposed for a short time. The Ss were instructed to recover the colors they had just seen from the chart of 120 colors. The findings revealed that Ss were better able to recover those colors which were of high codability than those colors of low codability.

In a study utilizing an interlanguage design, Joseph Casagrande (Carroll and Casagrande 1958) compared responses of Hopi and English-speaking children. In Hopi it is obligatory for speakers to include reference to the form of the object they are speaking about. That is, the verb used will contain a different stem depending upon whether the object spoken about is a long flexible object or a long rigid object or a flat flexible object. This obligatory category is similar in many ways to the categories of time and number which are obligatory in English. Almost without exception every English sentence must contain reference to both time and number. In the same way Hopi sentences must contain reference to the form of the object spoken about.

It has been repeatedly demonstrated that English-speaking children will respond earliest to color. Color, for some reason, is learned very early and dominates many classifications which children develop. On the basis of the obligatory category of form in Hopi, however, it was predicted that Hopi children would give preference to form. The experiment designed to test this hypothesis consisted of presenting the children with two objects which differed from each other in both form and color, e.g., a blue stick and a yellow rope. Then a third object was presented which resembled one of the original objects in color and one in form, e.g., a yellow stick. The children were simply instructed to select one of the original objects which best went with the third object. The results from a number of such series clearly demonstrated that Hopi children will group on the basis of form whereas English-speaking children will group on the basis of color.

Both of these studies involved very small behavioral differences. Certainly selecting colors from a chart and grouping objects are relatively insignificant behaviors in themselves. But the implications of such studies extend well beyond the specific behaviors with which they deal. The implication is simply that language in both its lexical and syntactic aspects exerts an influence on nonlinguistic behavior. It remains for future research to spell out in detail what grammatical aspects exert influence and what behaviors are so influenced and in what ways such influence is manifested.

Utilizing a frame of reference similar in many respects to Whorf but concentrating on different codes within a single language, Basil Bernstein (1961) has advanced an influential and provocative hypothesis, which asserts that there are two different codes within English—an elaborated code spoken by the middle class and a restricted code spoken by the working class. In the elaborated code there are many alternatives available, the choices which these speakers make are drawn from a relatively large stock. Their language is therefore less predictable. Also, in the elaborated code a speaker's intentions are made explicit. In the restricted code, on the other hand, there are relatively few options; the choices are restricted to a relatively narrow range of alternatives. His language, consequently, is relatively easy to predict. And, unlike the elaborated code speaker, his intentions are seldom made explicit or elaborated.

One specific difference between these codes might make this hypothesis clearer. In the restricted code, when the child asks "why" the "reason" he gets is often only the conclusion. When he asks, for example, why he must go to bed, the working class mother is more likely to simply state her conclusion, "get to bed." The middle class mother, on the other hand, is more likely to give specific reasons, for example, you need your sleep, you must get up early tomorrow, and so on. Normally, the dialog between child and middle class mother lasts a lot longer than it does for the working class child and mother. This difference, according to Bernstein, has important implications for the development of language and cognition. When the child is given reasons he is being exposed to sequences and connections among thoughts, and these facilitate learning and reinforce curiosity. Such dialog exposes the child to new and different language stimuli to which he learns to respond appropriately. The working class child, however, is not so exposed, and consequently his curiosity is inhibited, his range of language stimulation is restricted.

Exactly what implications such hypotheses will have for language learning in general and for various cultural differences within language is not clear at the present time. In fact, it is not even clear what implications these hypotheses, formulated on the basis of British English, will have for American English. A great deal of research, however, is currently being directed at this question (for example, Williams and Naremore 1969; Williams 1970b), and the next few years should see this hypothesis concretized considerably and its implications for language and cognitive development made clear.

The obvious other half of this question of language differences or language relativity is, of course, language universality. That is, what features do all natural languages have in common? The nature and importance of language universals are clearly articulated by Greenberg, Osgood, and Jenkins (Greenberg 1966, p. xv):

Language universals are by their very nature summary statements about characteristics or tendencies shared by all human speakers. As such they constitute the most general laws of a science of linguistics (as contrasted with a method and a set of specific descriptive results). Further, since language is at once both an aspect of individual behavior and an aspect of human culture, its universals provide both the major point of contact with underlying psychological principles (psycholinguistics) and the major source of implications for human culture in general (ethnolinguistics).

The following brief sampling (all taken from Greenberg 1966) should provide some idea of the nature of language universals and of the varied ways in which they are conceived and formulated:

Every human language has proper names. (p. 21) If a language has a vowel system, it has contrasts of tongue height in that system. (p. 27) When the descriptive adjective precedes the noun, the demonstrative and the numeral, with overwhelmingly more than chance frequency, do likewise. (p. 86) All languages have pronominal categories involving at least three persons and two numbers. (p. 96) If a language has gender categories in the noun, it has gender categories in the pronoun. (p. 96) The term *taboo* is of Polynesian origin, and the very fact that we use such an exotic word to denote a phenomenon which is very common in our own culture is symptomatic of the universality of taboo. (p. 245)

In this all too brief account an attempt was made to characterize rather than systematize or review psycholinguistic research. Much has been left out. Many psycholinguists, for example, would consider research on speech pathologies, speech perception, bilingualism, second-language learning, the language of the deaf, the learning of reading, reading difficulties, and various other topics to be essentially psycholinguistic. But whether one chooses to view psycholinguistics broadly as the study of speech and language psychology in general or narrowly as the study of sentence encoding and decoding seems unimportant. What does seem important is that psycholinguistics has much to contribute to our understanding of speech, language, and behavior in all its aspects.

REFERENCES

BERLYNE, D. E. 1966. Mediating responses: a note on Fodor's criticism. *Journal of Verbal Learning and Verbal Behavior* 5: 408–411.

BERNSTEIN, B. B. 1961. Social class and linguistic development: a theory of social learning, in *Education, economy and society*, Halsey, A. H., Floud, J., and Anderson, A., eds. New York: Harcourt, Brace & World, 288–314.

BEVER, T. G. 1968. Associations to stimulus-response theories of language, in *Verbal behavior and general behavior theory*, Dixon, T. R., and Horton, D. L., eds. Englewood Cliffs, New Jersey: Prentice-Hall, 478–494.

BLANKENSHIP, J., and KAY, C. 1964. Hesitation phenomena in English speech: a study in distribution. *Word* 20: 360–372.

BLUMENTHAL, A. L. 1970. *Language and psychology: historical aspects of psycholinguistics.* New York: Wiley.

———., and BOAKES, R. 1967. Prompted recall of sentences. *Journal of Verbal Learning and Verbal Behavior* 6: 674–676.

BOUCHER, J., and OSGOOD, C. E. 1969. The Pollyanna hypothesis. *Journal of Verbal Learning and Verbal Behavior* 8: 1–8.

BOWERS, J. W. 1970. Content analysis, in *Methods of research in communication*, Emmert, P., and Brooks, W. D., eds. Boston: Houghton Mifflin, 291–314.

BROWN, R., and LENNEBERG, E. H. 1954. A study in language and cognition. *Journal of Abnormal and Social Psychology* 49: 454–462.

CARROLL, J. B., ed. 1956. *Language, thought and reality: selected writings of Benjamin Lee Whorf.* New York: Wiley.

———. 1964. *Language and thought.* Englewood Cliffs, New Jersey: Prentice-Hall.

———., and CASAGRANDE, J. B. 1958. The function of language classifications in behavior, in *Readings in Social Psychology.* 3rd ed., Maccoby, E. E., Newcomb, T. M., and Hartley, E. L., eds. New York: Holt, Rinehart and Winston. 18–31.

CHOMSKY, N. 1957. *Syntactic structures.* The Hague: Mouton.

———. 1959. Review of B. F. Skinner's *Verbal behavior. Language* 35: 26–58.

———. 1965. *Aspects of the theory of syntax.* Cambridge: M.I.T. Press.

———. 1968. *Language and mind.* New York: Harcourt, Brace & World.

D'ARCAIS, G. B. F., and LEVELT, W. J. M., eds. 1970. *Advances in psycholinguistics.* New York: American Elsevier.

DARNELL, D. K. 1970. Semantic differentiation, in *Methods of research in communication*, Emmert, P., and Brooks, W. D., eds. Boston: Houghton Mifflin, 181–196.

DEVITO, J. A. Cloze procedure. 1967a. *Today's Speech* 15: 31–32.

———. 1967b. The meaning of psycholinguistics. *Today's Speech* 15: 19–22.

———. 1967c. Style and stylistics: an attempt at definition. *Quarterly Journal of Speech* 53: 248–255.

———. 1969a. Are theories of stuttering necessary? *Central States Speech Journal* 20: 170–177.

———. 1969b. Some psycholinguistic aspects of active and passive sentences. *Quarterly Journal of Speech* 55: 401–406.

———. 1970a. *The psychology of speech and language: an introduction to psycholinguistics*. New York: Random House.

———. 1970b. The verification of yes/no questions. Unpublished manuscript.

———. In press. Psycholinguistics and general semantics: some conceptual problems and resolutions, in *Research designs in general semantics*, Johnson, K. G., ed. Washington: Gordon and Breach.

———. In press b. Speech and language acquisition and development: a bibliography. *Bibliographic Annual in Speech Communication*.

ERVIN-TRIPP, S., and SLOBIN, D. I. 1966. Psycholinguistics. *Annual Review of Psychology* 17: 435–474.

FILLENBAUM, S. 1971. Psycholinguistics. *Annual Review of Psychology* 22: 251–308.

FLESHLER, H. 1969. The effects of varying sequences of audience attentiveness-inattentiveness on non-sequential features of speaker behavior. Unpublished Ph.D. dissertation. Pennsylvania State University.

FODOR, J. A. 1965. Could meaning be an $r_m$? *Journal of Verbal Learning and Verbal Behavior* 4: 73–81.

———. 1966. More about mediators: a reply to Berlyne and Osgood. *Journal of Verbal Learning and Verbal Behavior* 5: 412–415.

———., JENKINS, J. J., and SAPORTA, S. 1967. Psycholinguistics and communication theory, in *Human communication theory: original essays*, Dance, F. E. X., ed. New York: Holt, Rinehart, and Winston, 160–201.

GARRETT, M., BEVER, T. G., and FODOR, J. A. 1966. The active use of grammar in speech perception. *Perception and Psychophysics* 1: 30–32.

GARRETT, M., and FODOR, J. A. 1968. Psychological theories and linguistic constructs, in *Verbal behavior and general behavior theory*, Dixon, T. R., and Horton, D. L., eds. Englewood Cliffs, New Jersey: Prentice-Hall, 451–476.

GOLDMAN-EISLER, F. 1968. *Psycholinguistics: experiments in spontaneous speech.* New York: Academic Press.

GOUGH, P. B. 1965. Grammatical transformations and speed of understanding. *Journal of Verbal Learning and Verbal Behavior* 4: 107–111.

———. 1966. The verification of sentences: the effects of delay of evidence and sentence length. *Journal of Verbal Learning and Verbal Behavior* 5: 492–496.

GREENBERG, J. H., ed. 1966. *Universals of language.* 2nd ed. Cambridge: M.I.T. Press.

———., and JENKINS, J. J. 1964. Studies in the psychological correlates of the sound system of American English. *Word* 20: 157–177.

———., OSGOOD, C. E., and JENKINS, J. J. 1966. Memorandum concerning language universals, in *Universals of language.* 2nd ed. Greenberg, J. H., ed. Cambridge: M.I.T. Press, xv–xxvii.

HÖRMANN, H. 1971. *Psycholinguistics: An introduction to research and theory*, trans. H. H. Stern. New York: Springer -Verlag.

JAKOBOVITS, L. A., and MIRON, M. S., eds. 1967. *Readings in the psychology of language.* Englewood Cliffs, New Jersey: Prentice-Hall.

JAKOBSON, R. 1960. Closing statement: linguistics and poetics, in *Style in language*, Sebeok, T. A., ed. Cambridge: M.I.T. Press.

KATZ, J. J., and POSTAL, P. 1964. *An integrated theory of linguistic descriptions.* Cambridge: M.I.T. Press.

LEREA, L. 1956. A preliminary study of the verbal behavior of speech fright. *Speech Monographs* 23: 229–233.

LOUNSBURY, F. 1965. Pausal, juncture, and hesitation phenomena, in *Psycholinguistics: a survey of theory and research problems*, Osgood, C. E., and Sebeok, T. A., eds. Bloomington: Univ. of Indiana Press, 98–101.

LYNCH, M. D. 1970. Stylistic analysis, in *Methods of research in communication*, Emmert, P., and Brooks, W. D., eds. Boston: Houghton Mifflin, 315–342.

LYONS, J., ed. 1970. *New horizons in linguistics.* Baltimore: Penguin Books.

MACLAY, H., and OSGOOD, C. E. 1959. Hesitation phenomena in spontaneous English speech. *Word* 15: 19–44.

MCCROSKEY, J. C., and MEHRLEY, R. S. 1969. The effect of disorganization on attitude change and source credibility. *Speech Monographs* 36: 13–21.

McNEILL, D. 1966. Developmental psycholinguistics, in *The genesis of language: a psycholinguistic approach,* Smith, F., and Miller, G. A., eds. Cambridge: M.I.T. Press, 15–84.

———. 1970. *The acquisition of language: the study of developmental psycholinguistics.* New York: Harper & Row.

MAHL, G. F. 1956. Disturbances and silences in the patient's speech in psychotherapy. *Journal of Abnormal and Social Psychology* 53: 1–15.

MAHL, G. G., and SCHULZE, G. 1964. Psychological research in the extralinguistic area, in *Approaches to semiotics, transactions of the Indiana University conference on paralinguistics and kinesics,* Sebeok, T. A., Hayes, A. S., and Bateson, M. C., eds. The Hague: Mouton, 51–124.

MARKEL, N. N., ed. 1969. *Psycholinguistics: an introduction to the study of speech and personality.* Homewood, Ill.: Dorsey Press.

MENYUK, P. 1971. *The acquisition and development of language.* Englewood Cliffs, New Jersey: Prentice-Hall.

MESSER, S. 1967. Implicit phonology in children. *Journal of Verbal Learning and Verbal Behavior* 6: 455–460.

MILLER, G. A. 1962. Some psychological studies of grammar. *American Psychologist* 17: 748–762.

———., and McNEILL, D. 1969. Psycholinguistics, in *The handbook of social psychology.* 2nd ed., vol. 3, Lindzey, G., and Aronson, E., eds. Reading, Mass.: Addison-Wesley, 666–794.

MIRON, M. S. 1961. A cross-linguistic investigation of phonetic symbolism. *Journal of Abnormal and Social Psychology* 62: 623–630.

MORRIS, C. 1958. Words without meaning: review of B. F. Skinner's *Verbal behavior. Contemporary Psychology* 3: 212–214.

MOWRER, O. H. 1960. *Learning theory and the symbolic processes.* New York: Wiley.

NEWMAN, S. 1933. Further experiments in phonetic symbolism. *American Journal of Psychology* 45: 53–75.

NUNNALLY, J. C. 1965. Individual differences in word usage, in *Directions in psycholinguistics,* Rosenberg, S., ed. New York: Macmillan, 203–234.

OGILVIE, M., and DeVITO, J. A. In press. The training of the language clinician or teacher, in *Language development, the key to learning,* Jones, M. V., ed. Springfield, Ill.: Charles C. Thomas.

OSGOOD, C. E. 1958. A question of sufficiency: review of B. F. Skinner's *Verbal behavior. Contemporary Psychology* 3: 209–212.

———. 1963a. On understanding and creating sentences. *American Psychologist* 18: 735–751.

———. 1963b. Psycholinguistics, in *Psychology: a study of a science*, vol. 6, Koch, S., ed. New York: McGraw-Hill, 244–316.

———. 1966. Meaning cannot be an $r_m$? *Journal of Verbal Learning and Verbal Behavior* 5: 402–407.

———. 1968. Toward a wedding of insufficiencies, in *Verbal behavior and general behavior theory*, Dixon, T. R., and Horton, D. L., eds. Englewood Cliffs, New Jersey: Prentice-Hall, 495–519.

———., SUCI, G., and TANNENBAUM, P. H. 1957. *The measurement of meaning*. Urbana: Univ. of Illinois Press.

———., and WALKER, E. G. 1959. Motivation and language behavior: a content analysis of suicide notes. *Journal of Abnormal and Social Psychology* 59: 58–67.

ROMMETVEIT, R. 1968. *Words, meanings, and messages: theory and experiments in psycholinguistics*. New York: Academic Press.

ROSENBERG, S., and KOPLIN, J. H., eds. 1968. *Developments in applied psycholinguistics research*. New York: Macmillan.

SANFORD, F. H. 1942. Speech and personality: a comparative case study. *Character and Personality* 10: 169–198.

SAPIR, E. 1929. A study in phonetic symbolism. *Journal of Experimental Psychology* 12: 225–239.

SAPORTA, S., ed. 1961. *Psycholinguistics: a book of readings*. New York: Holt, Rinehart and Winston.

SAVIN, H. B., and PERCHONOCK, E. 1965. Grammatical structure and the immediate recall of English sentences. *Journal of Verbal Learning and Verbal Behavior* 4: 348–353.

SKINNER, B. F. 1957. *Verbal behavior*. New York: Appleton-Century-Crofts.

SLOANE, H. N. JR., and MACAULAY, B. D., eds. 1968. *Operant procedures in remedial speech and language training*. New York: Houghton Mifflin.

SLOBIN, D. I. 1971. *Psycholinguistics*. Glenview, Ill.: Scott, Foresman.

SMITH, O. W., and KOUTSTAAL, C. W. 1969. Additional correlates of Greenberg and Jenkins' linguistic S scale. *Psychological Reports* 24: 999–1002.

SNIDER, J. G., and OSGOOD, C. E., eds. 1969. *Semantic differential technique: a source-book*. Chicago: Aldine.

STOLZ, W. S., and TANNENBAUM, P. H. 1963. Effects of feedback on oral encoding behavior. *Language and Speech* 6: 218–228.

TAYLOR, I. K., and TAYLOR, M. M. 1962. Phonetic symbolism in four unrelated languages. *Canadian Journal of Psychology* 16: 344–356.

———. 1965. Another look at phonetic symbolism. *Psychological Bulletin* 64: 413–427.

TAYLOR, W. L. 1953. "Cloze" procedure: a new tool for measuring readability. *Journalism Quarterly* 30: 415–433.

———. 1956. Recent developments in the use of "cloze" procedure. *Journalism Quarterly* 33: 42–48, 99.

WILLIAMS, F. 1970a. Analysis of verbal behavior, in *Methods of research in communication*, Emmert, P., and Brooks, W. D., eds. Boston: Houghton Mifflin, 237–290.

———., ed. 1970b. *Language and poverty: perspectives on a theme.* Chicago: Markham.

———., and NAREMORE, R. C. 1969. On the functional analysis of social class differences in modes of speech. *Speech Monographs* 36: 77–102.

YNGVE, V. H. 1960. A model and an hypothesis for language structure. *Proceedings of the American Philosophical Society* 104: 444–466.

ZAJONC, R. B. 1968. Attitudinal effects of mere exposure. *Journal of Personality and Social Psychology, Monograph Supplement,* 9, part 2: 1–27.